WORLD MYTHOLOGY

ACHILLES

by Jason Glaser

Consultant:
Dr. Laurel Bowman
Department of Greek and Roman Studies
University of Victoria
Victoria, British Columbia

Capstone
press
Mankato, Minnesota

Capstone Press
151 Good Counsel Drive, P.O. Box 669, Mankato, Minnesota 56002
www.capstonepress.com

Library of Congress Cataloging-in-Publication Data
Glaser, Jason.
    Achilles / Jason Glaser; consultant, Laurel Bowman.
    p. cm.—(World mythology)
    Includes bibliographical references and index.
    ISBN 0-7368-2660-2 (hardcover)
    1. Achilles (Greek mythology)—Juvenile literature. [1. Achilles (Greek mythology)
2. Trojan War. 3. Mythology, Greek.] I. Title. II. Series: World mythology (Mankato, Minn.)
BL820.A22G58 2005
398.2'0938'02—dc22   2003027202

Summary: An introduction to Achilles and his place in Greek mythology, including his
connection with the Trojan War and such figures as Athena and Apollo.

Editorial Credits
Blake A. Hoena, editor; Juliette Peters, series designer; Patrick Dentinger, book designer
    and illustrator; Alta Schaffer and Wanda Winch, photo researchers; Eric Kudalis,
    product planning editor

Photo Credits
Art Resource, NY/Réunion des Musées Nationaux, 8; Scala, 12, 14
Bridgeman Art Library/Courtauld Institute Gallery, Somerset House, London, 18;
    Galleria degli Uffizi, Florence, Italy, 10; Giraudon/Lauros, 16; Giraudon/Musée
    des Beaux Arts, Pau, France, 4
Corbis/Karl Weatherly, 20; Sandro Vannini, cover

1 2 3 4 5 6 09 08 07 06 05 04

TABLE OF CONTENTS

Peter Paul Rubens painted *Achilles Defeating Hector*. This painting shows the heroes Achilles (left) and Hector (right) in battle. The goddess Athena hovers over them.

Achilles (uh-KIH-leez) was a mighty Greek hero. **Ancient** Greeks and Romans told many stories about him. The stories said that Achilles could not be harmed. He was **invulnerable**.

The stories also said that gods helped Achilles and other heroes. During one battle, a hero named Hector threw his spear at Achilles. The goddess Athena (uh-THEE-nuh) knocked the spear down. Then Achilles raised his spear to throw at Hector. But the god Apollo created a fog around Hector. Achilles could not see Hector.

Hector ran from Achilles. As Hector ran, Athena approached him. She had **disguised** herself as one of his brothers. So Hector stopped. Athena offered him a new spear, but it was a trick. When Hector reached for the spear, it disappeared.

Achilles then caught up to Hector. He attacked and killed Hector. Achilles defeated many enemies in battle.

GREEK *and* ROMAN *Mythical Figures*

Greek Name: **APOLLO**
Roman Name: **APOLLO**
God of youth, music, and healing

Greek Name: **ATHENA**
Roman Name: **MINERVA**
Goddess of wisdom and protector of heroes

Greek Name: **HECTOR**
Roman Name: **HECTOR**
Leader of the Trojan army

Greek Name: **HELEN**
Roman Name: **HELEN**
Menelaus' wife

Greek Name: **HEPHAESTUS**
Roman Name: **VULCAN**
God of fire

Greek Name: **MENELAUS**
Roman Name: **MENELAUS**
Greek king married to Helen

Greek Name: **ODYSSEUS**
Roman Name: **ULYSSES**
Greek hero

Greek Name: **PARIS**
Roman Name: **PARIS**
Trojan prince who stole Helen from Menelaus and killed Achilles

Greek Name: **PATROCLUS**
Roman Name: **PATROCLUS**
Achilles' friend

Greek Name: **THETIS**
Roman Name: **THETIS**
Achilles' mother

6

Ancient Greeks and Romans believed in many gods. They told about the gods in stories called myths. Myths said the gods made the world and everything in it.

People honored and worshipped the gods. They believed they would be kept safe if they pleased the gods. People also believed they would be punished if they made the gods angry. In one story, the goddess Athena made the Greek hero Ajax go insane. Ajax had broken one of her statues.

Myths said the gods helped people. *The Iliad* is a long poem by the Greek poet Homer. *The Iliad* is nearly 3,000 years old. It tells about the last year of the **Trojan** War. During this war, a Greek army captured the city of Troy. In *The Iliad,* gods helped both the Greek and Trojan armies.

Ancient Greeks and Romans liked to tell the story of *The Iliad*. Many great heroes fought and died in the Trojan War. One of the greatest heroes was Achilles.

On this ancient Greek vase, Achilles (left center) is shown with his mother (right center). Ancient Greeks decorated everyday items like vases, cups, and bowls with scenes from myths.

ACHILLES' BIRTH

Achilles' mother was Thetis (THEE-tuhss). She was a sea **nymph**. Nymphs were creatures that never grew old or died. They were **immortal**. Achilles' father was the human King Peleus (PEE-lee-uhss). Peleus ruled an area of Greece called Phthia (THYE-uh). Because Achilles was part human, he would grow old and die. He was **mortal**.

Thetis wanted to keep Achilles from dying of old age. At night, Thetis put Achilles into a fire to burn off his mortal skin. In the morning, she rubbed ambrosia (am-BROH-zhuh) on him to heal his body. Ambrosia was the food of the gods.

Achilles' mother also wanted to protect her son from harm. Thetis held Achilles by the heel and dipped him into the river Styx. This river ran through the **Underworld**. Its waters made Achilles invulnerable. The water covered Achilles everywhere but the heel that Thetis held. Achilles' heel was the only part of his body that could be harmed.

Achilles at the Court of King Lycomedes with His Daughters was painted by Pompeo Girolamo Batoni. This painting shows Achilles (left) dressed as a woman and holding a sword.

THE TROJAN WAR

The Trojan War began when Trojan Prince Paris took Helen from her husband. Helen was married to Greek King Menelaus (meh-nuh-LAY-uhss). Menelaus gathered an army to go get Helen back. He needed help from heroes like Achilles.

Thetis did not want Achilles to join the Greek army. She was afraid her son would die in the Trojan War. Thetis dressed Achilles as a woman and sent him to hide on the island of Scyros.

Menelaus told the wise hero Odysseus (oh-DIH-see-uhss) to find Achilles. Odysseus sailed to Scyros. He had heard that Achilles was hiding among King Lycomedes' (lye-koh-MEE-deez) daughters. Lycomedes ruled Scyros.

Odysseus played a trick on Achilles. He set out treasures and a sword. The king's daughters looked at the treasures, but Achilles looked at the sword. Odysseus then knew which woman was actually Achilles. Odysseus talked Achilles into going to Troy and helping the Greek army.

The Fury of Achilles, painted by Charles-Antoine Coypel, shows Achilles (center) in battle. Athena is to the left of Achilles. The sea god Poseidon is to the right of Achilles.

Achilles killed many people in battle. On the way to Troy, he stopped on the island of Tenedos. King Tenes (TEN-eez) ruled the island. Thetis warned Achilles not to harm the king. But Achilles argued with Tenes and killed him. Achilles' actions angered the god Apollo. Apollo was Tenes' father.

During the Trojan War, Achilles fought the Trojan hero Cygnus (SIG-nuhss). Like Achilles, Cygnus was invulnerable to weapons. Achilles used the strap on Cygnus' helmet to choke him to death.

Priam (PRYE-uhm) was the king of Troy. One of his 50 sons was named Troilus (TROI-luhss). The gods had said Troilus would never lose a battle if he lived to be 20 years old. Achilles killed Troilus before he turned 20. Achilles killed many of Priam's sons.

Achilles also attacked the city of Lyrnessus. There, he captured a beautiful woman named Briseis (brih-SEE-ihss). Achilles and Briseis fell in love.

In *Euribates and Taltibius Lead Briseis before Agamemnon* by Giovanni Battista Tiepolo, Agamemnon (gold robe) waits for his men as they lead Briseis from Achilles' tent.

ACHILLES AND AGAMEMNON

Agamemnon (ay-guh-MEM-non) was the leader of the Greek army. He had captured Chryseis (kry-SEE-ihss). Chryseis' father asked the god Apollo to get his daughter back. Apollo told the Greeks to let Chryseis go. Achilles made Agamemnon give Chryseis back to her father.

Achilles' actions angered Agamemnon. Agamemnon took Briseis from Achilles. Achilles then became sad and would not leave his tent. He no longer wanted to fight the Trojans.

Achilles led the **Myrmidons** (MUR-muh-duhnss). These soldiers were ants that had been changed into men. Without Achilles and the Myrmidons, the Greek army lost many battles. They could not beat Hector, the leader of the Trojan army.

Achilles' friends begged him to fight. Agamemnon even returned Briseis. Achilles still refused to help. His mother, Thetis, had told Achilles that he would die if he stayed and fought. Achilles thought about going home.

Achilles (red cloak) stands over Patroclus in Giovanni Antonio Pellegrini's painting *Achilles Contemplating the Body of Patroclus.*

Patroclus (puh-TROH-kluhss) was Achilles' best friend. Patroclus did not want the Greeks to lose the war. He asked to use Achilles' **armor**. He also asked to lead the Myrmidons into battle. Achilles agreed to give Patroclus whatever he wanted. But Achilles did not want Patroclus to get hurt. He warned Patroclus only to push the Trojan army away from the Greek army's camp.

Patroclus disguised himself with Achilles' armor. When he entered the battle, the Greeks believed that Patroclus was Achilles. The Greeks began to fight harder because they thought Achilles was there to help them. They began to beat the Trojan army. The Trojans ran away from the Greek army's camp.

Patroclus forgot about Achilles' warning. He chased after the Trojans. Patroclus caught up to Hector, and the two heroes fought. Hector was strong. He also had help from Apollo. Hector killed Patroclus and took Achilles' armor.

The Death of Achilles was painted by Peter Paul Rubens. In this painting, Paris (left) holds the bow he used to shoot Achilles (center). Apollo hovers over Paris, guiding Paris' arrow into Achilles' heel.

Patroclus' death made Achilles angry. Achilles decided to stay and fight the Trojans. Thetis asked the gods to help her son. The god Hephaestus (he-FESS-tuhss) made Achilles new armor. Achilles then went looking for Hector.

Achilles killed dozens of Trojans in his search. After Achilles killed one of Hector's brothers, Hector agreed to fight. The two heroes fought hard, but Achilles was stronger. Athena also helped him. Achilles killed Hector.

With help from Achilles, the Greeks began to win more battles. The Trojans' weapons were useless against Achilles. But he did have a weakness.

During one battle, Prince Paris stood on top of Troy's walls. He shot an arrow at Achilles. The god Apollo saw a chance to get **revenge** for the death of his son Tenes. Apollo made the arrow hit Achilles' heel. Achilles' heel was not invulnerable like the rest of his body. He died from the wound.

The Achilles tendon stretches from people's heels to their calf muscles.

People thought Achilles could not be hurt, but Apollo knew his weakness. People sometimes use the expression "Achilles' heel" to describe a person's weakness. A person fighting a much stronger enemy will usually lose. But a person who can find an enemy's Achilles' heel, or weak spot, might win the battle.

The muscle near a person's heel is called the Achilles tendon. It is named after the spot where Achilles was hit by Paris' arrow. The Achilles tendon goes from the heel bone to the calf muscle. People sometimes hurt their Achilles tendon during work or sports. Injuries to this tendon can keep people from walking, running, or jumping.

Today, people no longer believe that Greek and Roman myths are true. But stories about gods and heroes are still popular. *The Iliad* has been printed into books. Movies have been made about popular myths. People continue to enjoy stories about Achilles and other famous heroes.

PLACES IN MYTH

Adriatic Sea

Black Sea

ITALY

GREECE

Phthia

TENEDOS

•Troy
•Lyrnessus

Aegean Sea

—SCYROS

ITHACA—

Ionian Sea

Athens

Sparta

LEGEND

• City

▲ Mount Olympus

CRETE

SCALE
Miles

0   100   200

0   100   200

Kilometers

Mediterranean Sea

GLOSSARY

ancient (AYN-shunt)—having lived a long time ago

armor (AR-mur)—protective covering, such as a helmet and a breastplate, worn by a soldier

disguise (diss-GIZE)—to hide your appearance with a costume

immortal (i-MOR-tuhl)—able to live forever

invulnerable (in-VUHL-nur-uh-buhl)—unable to be harmed

mortal (MOR-tuhl)—not able to live forever; humans are mortal.

Myrmidons (MUR-muh-duhnss)—skilled soldiers who once had been ants; the god Zeus turned the Myrmidons into men.

nymph (NIMF)—a female spirit or goddess found in a meadow, a forest, a sea, or a stream

revenge (rih-VENJ)—an action taken to cause harm to someone who has caused harm to you or someone you care about

Trojan (TROH-juhn)—a person from the ancient city of Troy, or having to do with the city of Troy, such as the Trojan War

Underworld (UHN-dur-wurld)—the place under the earth where spirits of the dead go

READ MORE

Hoena, B. A. *Odysseus.* World Mythology. Mankato, Minn.: Capstone Press, 2004.

Little, Emily. *Trojan Horse: How the Greeks Won the War.* Step into Reading. New York: Random House, 2003.

USEFUL ADDRESSES

**National Junior Classical
 League**
422 Wells Mill Drive
Miami University
Oxford, OH 45056

Ontario Classical Association
PO Box 19505
55 Bloor Street West
Toronto, ON M4W 3T9
Canada

INTERNET SITES

FactHound offers a safe, fun way to find Internet sites related to this book. All of the sites on FactHound have been researched by our staff.

Here's how:
1. Visit *www.facthound.com*
2. Type in this special code **0736826602** for age-appropriate sites. Or enter a search word related to this book for a more general search.
3. Click on the **Fetch It** button.

FactHound will fetch the best sites for you!

INDEX